12.40

398.2   Moore, R W9-AKW-442
Moo

Hercules

HERCULES

HERCULES

By ROBIN MOORE

ILLUSTRATIONS BY ALEXA RUTHERFORD

ALADDIN PAPERBACKS

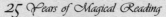

25 Years of Magical Reading

ALADDIN PAPERBACKS
EST. 1972

First Aladdin Paperbacks edition June 1997

Copyright © 1997 by Robin Moore
Illustrations © 1997 by Alexa Rutherford
Aladdin Paperbacks
An imprint of Simon & Schuster
Children's Publishing Division
1230 Avenue of the Americas
New York, NY 10020

Printed and bound in the United States of America
10 9 8 7 6 5 4 3 2
Library of Congress Cataloging-in-Publication Data
Hercules / by Robin Moore ; illustrations by Alexa Rutherford. — 1st
Aladdin Paperback ed.
p.   cm.
Summary: Retells the story of the legendary demi-god and his twelve tasks.
ISBN 0-689-81228-0 (hc). — ISBN 0-689-81229-9 (pbk.)
1. Heracles (Greek mythology)—Juvenile literature. [1. Hercules (Roman
mythology) 2. Mythology, Roman.] I. Rutherford, Alexa, ill. II. Title.
BL820.H5M66   1997
398.2'0938'01—DC20   96-42477
CIP   AC

A Boy Is Born

There was a time when Ancient Greece was covered with forests and swamps. Blood-thirsty robbers waited along the lonely roadways. Snakes swam in the muddy rivers. Savage beasts roamed the woods and slept in dripping caves.

In the midst of this dangerous time, a boy was born. His name was Alcides.

He was not like other boys. He was half-human and half-god.

His mother was the good Queen Alcmene. She came from a heroic family. Her grandfather was Perseus, the ancient warrior who slew the evil Medusa with his singing sword.

Alcmene gave Alcides the gift of a mother's love.

His father was Zeus, the mightiest of the Greek gods. He was called Gatherer of the Clouds and The One Who Hurls Thunderbolts. When thunder rumbled in the dark clouds and lightning sliced the sky, people knew that Zeus was near.

Zeus gave Alcides the gift of tremendous strength.

In those days, the gods and goddesses lived high on the misty top of Mount Olympus. They used their powers to change people's lives. Sometimes they helped them. Sometimes they harmed them. Sometimes they mystified them.

The goddess Hera was often angry. Her anger gave her great power. And her power made her cruel.

From the moment he was born, Alcides was in Hera's way. Even though he had done nothing to harm her, she hated the child. Hera was really angry at Zeus. But she knew the thunder god was more powerful than she was. So she turned her anger on Zeus's newborn son. She gave him a curse: a terrible temper. And she gave him no control over his temper.

When he was still a young baby, Alcides would wail and thrash about. His cries would fill the hallways. Even his mother could not shake him from these fits of rage.

Queen Alcmene took Alcides to the blind prophet Teiresias to have his fortune read. The old man told her about Hera's curse. Still the queen was not discouraged.

She had the scribes change her son's name to Hercules, which means "For

HERCULES

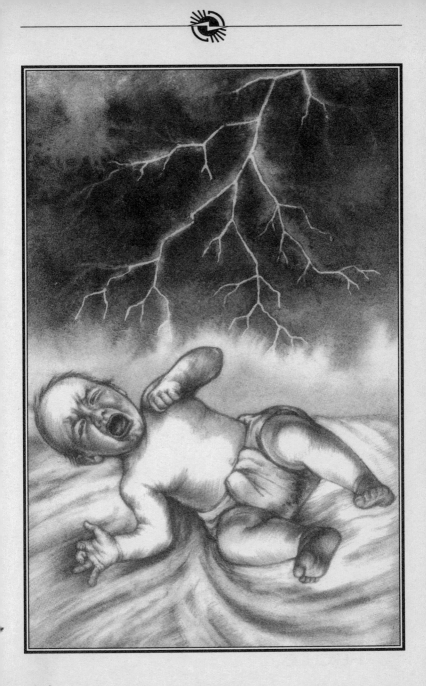

the Glory of Hera." She had them write his new name on their long scrolls for everyone to see. The good queen thought this might cool Hera's anger. But she was wrong.

That very evening, Hera made her first attempt to kill Hercules.

I t was a hot night, late in summer. The sky was clear and the stars were shining brightly. Hercules and his mother often slept on their flat roof. The house was on a slight hill within the walls of Thebes. Sometimes a cool ocean breeze would rise and blow away the simmering heat of the city.

That night, the queen laid Hercules in his cradle. Then she went to her own sleeping cot, a few feet away.

Hercules slept well. He did not know that Hera had sent two immense river snakes to interrupt his sleep. The snakes crawled up the drainpipes and slithered across the rooftop to the spot where the boy lay in his cradle.

They lifted their heads and flicked their forked tongues. They turned from side to side. Then they crawled into the cradle with Hercules and wound their coils around the baby's neck. He opened his mouth to cry, but no sound came out.

Hera had not counted on the child's astonishing strength. With his small

hands, Hercules tore the necklace of scaly coils from his throat. He held both serpents and squeezed his small fists, crushing their neck bones.

The snakes did not die right away. They thrashed about, whipping their tails against the side of the cradle. When Queen Alcmene heard the noise, she sprang from her bed. Two servants came, carrying flickering torches. But everyone could see that the danger was over.

Hercules dropped the snakes at his mother's feet. They lay like coils of rope.

Queen Alcmene stared at her son in wonder.

"It is true," she said. "You have the strength of Great Zeus within you!"

Hercules threw back his head and laughed.

3

HIS TRAINING

A s Hercules grew to manhood, his family did its best to prepare him for a life as a hero. His uncles taught him to handle a sword and spear.

Zeus watched Hercules from his mountaintop. He sent the gods in human form to train Hercules in archery, charioteering, and wrestling.

By the time he was eighteen, Hercules was the strongest and bravest man in all of Greece.

But he was not happy.

Just as the prophet had predicted, young Hercules flew into a rage again and again. He injured whoever came near him.

Soon, no other boy would play sports with him. No teacher would risk entering his room. Even his mother feared he might harm her in some careless way.

At last, the queen decided it would be best if Hercules left the city. She sent him off into the countryside of Thebes, to watch over the kingdom's sheep.

Hercules was sorry to leave his home. But he set off, eager to begin his first real adventure. His mother had told him he must protect their flock from wild beasts and robbers.

The countryside was not very interesting to Hercules. No wild beasts ventured near the flock. No robbers came.

Hercules spent his days alone in the hills. At night, he would wrap himself in a blanket, sit by the fire, and stare at the starry sky, just as he had when he and his mother slept on their roof.

On those lonely nights, he would often play a game he had taught himself as a small boy. He would arrange the stars into groups and stare at each group until it became a shape.

Sometimes the shape would be an animal, a goose or a bear. Sometimes it would be a person, like his great-grandfather, Perseus.

At night, when he went to sleep, Hercules was watched over by the stars.

4

His First Adventure

Early one morning, Hercules found a sheep from his flock lying dead on the hillside. Nearby, he saw the track of a lion. The print was so large that it took both of his outstretched hands to cover it. The smell of a lion rose from the trampled ground.

Hercules decided to go after the lion while the track was still fresh. He strung his cedarwood bow and tied his quiver of cane arrows onto his back. He checked that his bronze-bladed knife was ready at his belt.

Then he set off, following the lion's trail.

Once, weeks before, Herucles had heard stories about this beast. In the crowded marketplace outside the house of King Thespius, he had seen a large knot of people clustered around a white-haired man. The old man had only one tooth. But his tongue was clever and he had a memory like an open book. Every marketplace had a storyteller. And every storyteller knew the local terrors of the land.

Hercules had listened quietly as the old man explained that the big cat lived in a rocky cave on the slopes of nearby Mount Cithaeron. The ground outside the cave, he said, was littered with the bones of warriors and magicians who had tried to kill the beast.

Now Hercules was climbing that very mountain. As he reached its crest, the lion sprang from a cave and charged toward him, showing blood-stained teeth.

Reaching over his shoulder, Hercules drew an arrow and fit it to his bowstring. Just as the gods had taught him, he drew the string back until it touched his cheekbone. He aimed straight for the lion's chest and released the arrow.

It was a good shot, but the arrow did not kill the lion. Its skin was as tough as a metal shield, and the arrow bounced off and shattered against a nearby boulder.

Hercules was ready. He released another arrow, aimed at the beast's open mouth. But before the shaft could reach him, the lion leaped aside and landed lightly on its feet. Hercules watched as his arrow flew into a clump of bushes.

The Thespian Lion sat with his feet together and stared at Hercules. His eyes were the color of green fire.

Hercules stared back at the lion.

He felt a great strength welling up. Casting aside his bow, he sprang at the lion with his bare hands outstretched. At the same moment, the lion leaped at Hercules in a long, arching jump.

Hercules was quick. He caught the beast by the throat and spun behind him, locking his arms around his neck.

They landed hard and began rolling downhill. The lion tossed his head from side to side. He hunched his massive shoulders, trying to throw Hercules off.

But Hercules only tightened his grip. He squeezed the breath from the lion, just as he had with the river snakes. At last, they slid to a stop on the rocky mountainside and the shaggy beast went limp in Hercules' arms. The young hero let him fall to the ground.

As Hercules stood catching his breath, he looked down at the lion's body. He felt both proud and ashamed.

He had defeated an enemy of the kingdom. But he had destroyed something of great beauty. To remember this moment, he decided to take the beast's skin and wear it as a cloak.

Drawing his knife, Hercules began to work at the lion's skin. But he could not cut the thick hide. He found a sharp sliver of rock, but that did not work either.

Then Hercules noticed the lion's huge claws. Lifting the beast's leg, he sliced through the long and tawny hide, skinning the lion with its own claws.

Hercules threw the skin over his shoulders. The lion's head fit over his own like a helmet, with his face peering from the open mouth.

5

IN ATHENA'S TEMPLE

Y ou should have seen the villagers' faces when Hercules came walking out of the hills in his lion's skin. Their eyes grew wide and their mouths dropped open. They cheered and shouted, calling Hercules a great hero.

But he didn't stop to enjoy their praise. Instead, he went to the temple of the goddess Athena, in Thebes. Athena was the goddess of wisdom and bravery. She wore armor and carried a warrior's sword and shield.

If anyone could help lift Hera's curse, it would be Wise Athena.

Athena's temple sat in a grove of olive trees by a fast-flowing stream. Hercules knelt by a rocky waterfall and washed the lion's blood from his hands. Then he rose and stepped between the white marble columns, into the quiet of the temple.

Hercules knelt on the stone floor, closed his eyes, and prayed to the goddess.

"Why have you come?" a voice asked.

Hercules opened his eyes and saw Athena standing before him. She was just as the storytellers had described her. A shaft of sunlight glinted off her polished shield.

For a moment, Hercules was too astonished to speak. Then he found his voice.

"Help me lift Hera's curse," he said. "I carry it like a stone on my back."

Athena shook her head.

"I cannot lift the curse, Hercules. Only you have that power," she said.

"I don't understand."

Athena smiled. "You have come to a crossroads, Brave Hercules," she said. Her voice was like the sound of water, running over smooth stones. "You have learned a warrior's skills. You are fearless and strong. But will you use your bravery and strength to harm others? Or will you use it to serve your country?

"If you choose a life of service, I will help you stand against Hera's anger."

"I will do whatever you ask," said Hercules.

"Go to King Eurystheus of Mycenae in the land of Argines," Athena said. "Tell him you will perform twelve tasks for him. When these labors are completed, come and see me again."

6

HERCULES BEGINS
HIS LABORS

When Hercules arrived in Mycenae, King Eurystheus was waiting. Hera had visited him in a dream. She told the king that she would give him great powers if he would help her defeat the young hero. The King and Hera laid out twelve tasks so difficult and dangerous that no mortal man could perform them.

When Hercules was shown into the king's throne room, he was stunned by the wealth that lay piled about. Heaps of gold coins and precious jewels glistened in the torchlight. Marble statues of the gods and goddesses stared down at him. In the midst of all this booty, attended by two young slaves, sat the plump, bearded monarch, King Eurystheus.

The king looked down his nose at Hercules. "Your first task," he told Hercules, "is to hunt the Nemean Lion. He lives in the forest west of the city. Bring me his body."

Hercules nodded. This savage beast was even more famous than the Thespian Lion. The storytellers said he was the strongest and most blood-thirsty creature in all of Greece.

But he was not very watchful.

That very afternoon, Hercules surprised him in the forest. The lion had just eaten two very large men and a dozen hunting dogs. He was wandering by the river, looking for a place to take a nap.

Hercules dropped from a tree branch and landed on the lion's back.

The beast glanced over his shoulder. But before he could attack, Hercules seized him by the mane and twisted, snapping his neck bones.

When the lion slumped to the

ground, Hercules sighed in relief. He admired the animal's huge claws and sharp teeth. He was glad he had been able to catch the creature when he was drowsy and well-fed.

Hercules threw the limp body over his shoulder and headed back to see the King. When he arrived at Eurystheus's throne room, the ruler's eyes grew wide with fear. He had not expected Hercules to survive.

"I see you are victorious," said the king. He would not meet Hercules' gaze.

"Not all the tasks will be this easy, Hercules. You have many labors ahead of you. From this day forward, you will stay far outside the city walls. My counselors will carry messages between us. I will not speak with you again."

Hercules nodded. He knew the king was afraid of him.

7

MORE LABORS

The next task was much harder than the first. Hercules was to go to the Swamps of Lerna and defeat the Hydra, a monster with nine heads and the body of a snake.

Many brave warriors had tried to kill the Hydra. But they all had been swallowed whole. Every time one of the Hydra's heads was cut off, two more heads would grow back. The longer a warrior fought, the more outnumbered he was. The end was always the same.

Hercules knew he could not defeat the Hydra alone. He sought out his young nephew, Iolaus.

"How will we defeat this beast?" the boy asked.

"I will carry my long-bladed sword," Hercules answered, "and you will carry a burning torch. Each time I cut off one of the Hydra's heads, you will burn the bloody stump so it cannot grow back."

Iolaus smiled. "A good plan."

Hercules looked at his nephew.

"Are you afraid?" he asked.

Iolaus nodded. "Yes. But if I am with

you, we will be victorious."

Hercules glanced at the sun.

"Let us begin," he said. "I want to be out of the swamps by nightfall."

Iolaus made six long-handled torches by tying together the stalks of river reeds and soaking their tips in olive oil. Meanwhile, Hercules sharpened the long blade of his fighting sword with a stone. It would have to be as sharp as a razor to sever the Hydra's heads with one swing.

At the edge of the swamp, Iolaus lit his first torch. The others were in a bundle on his back. Hercules drew his sword. With the boy right behind him, Hercules stepped into the muddy water. It smelled bad, as if something had died there. Soon the water rose to their knees. With each step, the deep mud almost sucked their sandals from their feet.

As they waded further into the swamp, they saw broken weapons and pieces of armor lying in the mud. In a place where the water rose to their belts, they heard a hissing sound and the Hydra's huge form rose out of the water.

All nine heads reared up. All nine mouths opened, showing fang-like

teeth. All eighteen eyes glared down. Then the heads began whipping around, like the limbs of a tree in a mighty storm. Their hissing filled the ears of the two young warriors.

Suddenly, one head lashed out at Hercules.

He swung his sword. The sharpened blade sliced through the beast's neck. The head, jaws still opening and closing, fell into the water and sank. The severed neck splashed blood in every direction.

Iolaus darted forward and thrust his burning torch at the Hydra, turning the writhing neck into a sizzling stump.

For a moment, the massive beast shuddered in pain. Then pain turned to rage, and all eight heads swooped down on Hercules. The swordsman was ready.

Hercules waded up to the Hydra, swinging his sword in long, deadly arcs. The blade whistled into the air and sliced through the creature's slimy flesh.

One after another, the heads toppled into the muddy water. One by one, Iolaus turned the snaky necks into blackened, bubbling stumps. When his torch burned low, he lit a fresh one. Black, evil-smelling smoke rolled up and filled the air.

At last, the Hydra's headless body rolled onto its side and sank into the swamp. The water around it turned thick and dark with blood.

Hercules slid his sword into its sheath. Iolaus dipped his last torch into the water, snuffing out the flame.

The young boy wiped the soot from his face.

"Our ancestor, Great Perseus, would be proud of you today," said Hercules.

Iolaus began to smile. Then he winced and slapped his arm. A mosquito fell into the water and floated away.

"Time to leave the swamp,"

Hercules grinned. "The most blood-thirsty creatures of all are just coming out. But first, there is something I must do."

Hercules waded through the mud to the headless Hydra and dipped the point of each arrow into the Hydra's blood. From that time forward, his arrows were poison-tipped. Even a small wound from one would cause instant death.

Hercules and Iolaus were away from the swamps of Lerna by nightfall. Hercules was brave, but he was not foolish.

To prove he had completed his

task, Hercules took along one of the Hydra's severed heads. It hissed quietly for several hours. Then it was silent.

8

EVEN MORE LABORS

The Nemean Lion and the Hydra of Lerna each had been defeated in one day's time. But the next task took Hercules an entire year to accomplish.

The king's messenger told him to journey to Mount Cerynea and capture alive the Hind of Artemis, a beautiful deer with golden antlers. Hercules tracked the wondrous creature for months. But the deer was clever and

sure-footed and always managed to stay just ahead of him.

One day, Hercules surprised her while she was drinking from the Ister River. He snatched her up and tied her hooves together with a strong cord. Then he slung the deer over his shoulders and delivered her, alive and still kicking, to the king's messengers.

Many more adventures followed. Sometimes Iolaus accompanied Hercules, sometimes he went alone. Some of the tasks were hair-raising. Others were simply humiliating.

Once, King Eurystheus ordered

Hercules to clean out the stables of a neighboring monarch, King Augeas. Augeas was a slob. He had kept three thousand cattle in his barn for seven years and had never once cleaned away the manure. The barn was a mile long and over a hundred feet tall. It was a sight to behold.

Hercules smelled the barn before he saw it. King Augeas pushed aside the massive double doors and led his visitor inside. Hercules shook his head in disgust when he saw the stinking, steaming piles. They were as high as his shoulders.

It was not a very noble job for a

hero, but Hercules had no choice. Augeas ordered his servants to herd the cattle outside. Then he handed Hercules a shovel and nodded to the mounds of manure.

But Hercules did not plan to soil his lion's skin. Instead, he took his shovel to the banks of the nearby Alpheus River.

He dug a trench from the river to the barn. He made a canal, which carried the quickly flowing stream through the open doorway of the barn and out the other side. Then, he dug another trench back to the river.

Augeas was astonished. He had never seen such furious digging. It would have taken one hundred men all day to accomplish what Hercules had done in a single hour.

Hercules leaned on his shovel and watched as the rushing waters swept the filth from the barn, carrying it downstream. Then he handed the shovel to Augeas and turned his back on the smelly kingdom.

It took brave Hercules many years to complete the twelve tasks. He suffered long and hard. At times, his only comfort was the night sky. He would see Perseus and the other great shapes sprinkled among the stars and his spirit would be refreshed.

At last, Hercules completed all twelve labors. King Eurystheus was furious. He had no idea that Hercules would be so strong and inventive. Hera was even more furious. Hercules had overcome the terrible forces that she had set against him and returned in victory. They had no choice but to release him from the King's service.

9

ATHENA'S ADVICE

Hercules returned to Thebes, battle-weary but hopeful, and sought out the Temple of Athena. Once again, he knelt on the hard stone floor.

"Goddess," he said, "I have done all you have asked. Now, tell me, am I free from Hera's curse?"

He saw the goddess of Wisdom standing before him.

"I have spoken with Hera," the

goddess said, "and asked her to wash away the curse, just as you washed away the filth of Augeas' cattle."

"What did she say?"

"She said you must bear the curse until the end of time."

Hercules felt tears of desperation on his cheeks.

"But goddess," he said, "am I no better off than when I started?"

"You are much better off," Athena said, "because in completing these labors, you have done what no other man has ever done: You have become immortal. You are now a god, like your father, Zeus."

Hercules was not comforted.

"But what good does it do me?" he moaned. "I still bear Hera's curse. At least when I was mortal, I knew my suffering would end with death."

"Your suffering has made you wise," she said.

"You have the gift of great strength and power," the goddess continued. "Can you learn to control the anger that Hera throws upon you? That, Hercules, will be your most difficult labor. If you can do that, you will truly be one of the gods."

Without another word, Athena vanished. Hercules was alone in the temple. He bent his head and wept.

Hercules tried to lead a quiet life and follow Athena's advice. But again and again, without warning, he would fly into a terrible rage and destroy everything and everyone in his path. When his anger had passed, he would gaze in horror at the terrible work of his hands.

After these fits of madness, Hercules would return to the Temple of Athena. Each time, the goddess sent him back out into the world. Hercules spent years in service to Grecian kings as a way of paying for his crimes.

In the midst of this hardship, the goddess of wisdom brought a ray of hope into Hercules' life.

One day, after competing in a wrestling contest, Hercules won the hand of a beautiful woman named Deianira. Like Hercules, she was strong and brave. But she was not controlled by Hera's anger. When Hercules was with her, he always felt calm and peaceful.

Unlike other women, Deianira was not afraid of Hercules' brute strength. She loved him with all her heart. She took him far away from cities and towns, to the very edge of the land. There they built a house beside the ocean.

At night they would sit on the rocky

beach, watching the stars rise over the sea, and listening to the soothing sound of the waves. Hercules pointed out the constellations he had found so long ago. For the first time, he was sharing them with another human being.

It seemed to Hercules that the love of this mortal woman had washed away Hera's curse.

10

THE GIFT OF THE ROBE

But Hera was not so easily defeated. She decided to use the love of his wife as a weapon against Hercules.

Hera looked into Deianira's heart and saw a weakness: She was painfully jealous of other women. This was one reason Deianira had taken her husband away from civilization. Out by the sea, she had him to herself.

One stormy summer night, Hera

came to Deianira in a dream. She told her that Hercules had fallen in love with another woman, younger and more lovely than Deianira.

Hercules' wife frowned and tossed in her sleep.

Then Hera spoke again, telling Deianira that if she wanted Hercules to be hers forever, she must use a love potion made from the blood of a centaur. Hera promised that as soon as the magical ointment touched Hercules' skin, he would never again look at another woman.

When Deianira woke, she found a bowl filled with centaur's blood at her bedside. That day, while Hercules was out, she took a length of fine cloth and sewed it into a magnificent robe.

She decorated it with drawings of Hercules' many victories. On the left breast, closest to his heart, she drew a picture of their house, with the ocean waves washing up by the door. Then she painted the inside of the robe with the potion. She hung it to dry in the breeze.

When Hercules returned, she placed the folded robe into his hands.

"I give you this gift," she said, "as a token of my love."

Hercules unfolded the robe and

held it up in the sunlight.

"This is better than my lion's skin!" he said.

He wrapped himself in the robe and smiled.

But his smile quickly vanished. His body twisted in pain. Tongues of yellow flame lifted the edges of the garment.

In that instant, Deianira understood she had been tricked. This was not a love potion—it was a fiery poison!

Hercules tried to tear the robe from his body, but the scalding liquid had glued the cloth to his skin. He turned and dashed into the ocean. He dove

and swam in the rolling waves, but the fire of Hera's potion still burned. Clouds of steam billowed around him and covered the beach in a thick fog.

Through the mist, Hercules saw Deianira swimming toward him. He felt his anger rising, and began to swim in her direction.

When they met, he reached for her throat with his deadly hands. He would choke her, just as he had the river snakes, and take his revenge for this terrible trick she had played.

But the look in his wife's eyes stopped him. Even with his powerful hands around her neck, she did not look afraid. Her eyes were filled with sorrow, but no fear. She was speaking to him, but he could not hear her above the roar of the waves.

Hercules had never before stopped himself from killing something. But he turned and dove deep, swimming for shore. He splashed through the surf and ran away. He wanted to get as far from Deianira as he could. He knew this was the only way she would be safe.

Hercules ran into the hills, howling like a mad beast.

In his agony, he thought he heard the sound of Hera's cruel laughter.

11

THE FIERY END

Then he heard the rumbling of thunder. When he lifted his eyes, he saw his father, Great Zeus himself, driving his golden chariot through the blue and crimson clouds.

His horses were the color of midnight. His eyes flashed under bushy eyebrows.

"Enough!" Zeus shouted. His voice echoed like a thunderclap through the hills.

Zeus wheeled his chariot up to his son and pulled his speeding horses to a stop. They snorted and reared. But the great god held them firmly by the reins. Overhead, the sky rumbled and flashed with jagged bolts of lightning.

Zeus lifted his right hand and pointed with a long and steady finger. Hercules saw his nephew, Iolaus, standing at the top of a hill. In his hand was a flaming torch. Beside him was a huge pile of dried wood. Iolaus bent and touched his torch to the branches. Flames swept the pile, throwing a shower of sparks into the sky.

Hercules turned back to Zeus. While

Hera's potion burned and bubbled against his skin, he forced himself to look into his father's face. The eyes of the thunder god were hard. But they were not cruel. Zeus nodded toward the crackling fire.

Hercules climbed the hill and approached the blazing pile. Hera's poison was burning him as badly as ever. But Zeus' bonfire felt even hotter. He saw Iolaus in the firelight, and raised his hand in farewell. Then he gave a great cry and hurled himself into the flames.

At first, Hercules felt no change. But then he felt the robe of Hera's deceit

loosening and falling away. He was surrounded by the white flames of Zeus.

Hercules rose with the heat of the flames. They carried him upward, above the treetops and scattered hills, into the thunderclouds.

Hercules felt the mist of the clouds on his face. The scorching fire was only a memory. He was cool and serene.

He rose higher and higher, until even Mount Olympus was far below him. The earth was a spinning ball in the blackened sky. Hercules looked about him. He was in a place of great distance and silence. He had reached the height of the stars.

Far away, Hercules could make out the shape of his great-grandfather Perseus outlined in the stars. He saw other constellations he remembered from his sheep-herding days.

He realized then that Zeus had placed him among the stars, where Hera's anger could not reach him.

This story happened long ago. The glory of ancient Greece is only a memory now. The old storytellers are silent. The great city of Thebes is a pile of rubble. The Temple of Athena is nothing but a ruin. And people do not worship the Greek gods and goddesses as they once did.

But you can still see Hercules' constellation in the night sky. He gazes down on Earth each evening.

Look for him tonight.

AUTHOR'S NOTE

N ow that you know Hercules' story, you might want to look for his constellation. Use the star chart at the back of this book and see if you can find the hero of the night sky. Once you have located him, you might be interested in learning more about the other constellations.

Of the eighty-eight constellations recognized by the International Astronomical Union in 1930, forty-nine are based on characters from the

Greek myths. Among these mythological figures, with the exception of Zeus, Hercules has the most constellations related to him. There are seven star groups that share his story: Aries, Cancer, Centaur, Draco, Hydra, Perseus, and Sagittarius.

Truly, Hercules was befriended by the stars.

FIND THE HERCULES CONSTELLATION IN THREE EASY STEPS:

1. **Locate the Big Dipper:**

   Look to the North Star—Polaris. The Big Dipper is nearby and easy to spot.

2. **Find the constellation Boötes—The Herdsman:**

   The three stars in the handle of the Big Dipper form a curve. If you follow the line of the handle away from the dipper, you will see a bright star, Arcturus, which is in the constellation Boötes.

3. **Locate Hercules:**

   Look to the east of Boötes to see the four "keystone" stars at the center of Hercules. You found him!

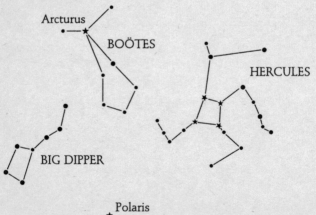

Want to find out more about the constellations? Get a star book from the library or bookstore and have fun exploring the night sky!